MOOSE WATCHERS HANDBOOK

Introduction

Much has changed since friend and publisher Dick Lemke of Impact New England, took the risk of publishing my Maine Moose Watchers Guide in 1993 in response to the growing interest in these largest of the deer in the world that had recently become so plentiful in the north woods of Maine.

- Moose watching territory in New England has expanded. New Hampshire and Vermont both have healthy moose herds whose members show themselves with predictability at certain locations. Servicing the thousands of folks who come to New England's north woods to see one of these gnarly-looking but generally gentle monsters has become big business.
- Moose watching interest has also grown tremendously at other select places in North America. Indeed, so many people have such fascination for these animals that I'm tempted to interview a psychiatrist about the reasons why. Tempted to, but afraid of the answers.
- Moose are more wary due to increased hunting pressure in some areas. Behavior changes due to increased interaction with moose watchers have also occurred. Accordingly, moose watchers need to be more savvy.

Thousands of folks come to New England's north woods to see one of these gnarly-looking but generally gentle monsters

Due to all of these factors it seems time for a Moose Watcher's Handbook. Knowing more about moose makes watching them all the more fun, as you have a better idea of what's going on. More importantly, knowing more about moose helps you to anticipate what that thousand or so pound animal in front of you might do next - like amble up to you!

The information for this book comes from a variety of sources. Some of it comes from interviewing moose watching enthusiasts. Some was provided by professional wildlife managers around the region, who willingly shared their research so that you could enjoy more moose. Most of it comes from the additional knowledge I've gained from meeting another thousand or so moose since 1993.

We offer it all to you here in the Moose Watcher's Handbook. We hope that it will enhance your enjoyment while seeking moose to watch wherever you may find them.

The behavior of any moose you might encounter is the responsibility of both you and the moose. Always remember that they are wild animals that can have their own bad hair days too

A mature bull stands about 7 feet at the shoulder. Add another 3 feet, with his head up, to the top of his antlers and you have a pretty awesome sight. Remember that the next time you stand under a regulation basketball rim

Moose completely submerge their head and sometimes their whole body in lakes and ponds

And bring up the aquatic vegetation that grows on the bottom, which they dearly love

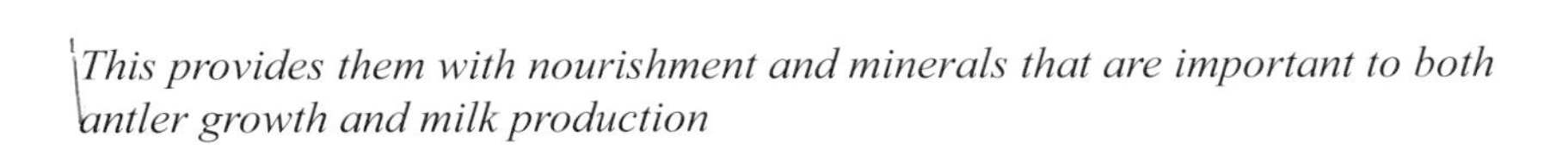

This provides them with nourishment and minerals that are important to both antler growth and milk production

What Exactly Is A Moose?

To get the most enjoyment out of watching any wildlife species it helps to know something about them. When it comes to an animal as large and powerful as a moose, it's also a very good idea. While most moose are normally quite gentle, some can get pretty darned mean. Informed moose watchers enjoy not only better experiences, but also safer ones, for both themselves and the moose.

What exactly is a moose? Let's look at some of the questions rookie moose watchers have asked me over the years before we try to answer that one.

What Family Of Animals Does The Moose Belong To?

Moose are actually deer. Their relatives include the elk, the caribou, the mule deer and the white-tailed deer all also found in North America. Moose are in fact the largest deer in the world. And moose inhabit a lot more of the world than one might think. They also live in Europe and Russia. While those moose are called elk, they are all moose at heart.

Why do the animals living in North America have a different name? Because the Indians native to this continent gave the moose its North American name. Moose means "twig eater" in the Algonquin language. That name provides a clue to one of the more important things that a moose watcher should know.

What Do Moose Eat?

Moose eat the twig ends of trees, and with tastes that cover a wide variety of trees. Mountain ash, maple, birch and balsam fir are all part of their diet.

They also eat the leaves and sometimes the bark of trees. And they love aquatic vegetation as well. Pondweed, water lily, arrowhead and such underwater delicacies provide moose with nourishment and minerals that are important to both antler growth and milk production.

But if you're worried about being attacked by a moose as a food source, you're safe. Moose are not carnivorous.

And for those who have speculated while watching a moose repeatedly submerge its head in some pond about how many fish a moose eats in a day, here's the fact: moose do not eat fish. What they're doing is eating vegetation off of the bottom.

How Big Is A Moose?

A mature bull moose of the subspecies Alces alces americana, commonly called the Canadian moose, stands over 7 feet tall at the shoulders. Its legs might be 40 inches long. The adult moose measures about 10 feet long from the end of its nose to the tip of its tail.

The average mature Canadian bull weighs from about 1000 to 1200 pounds, and can weigh as much as 1400 pounds or more. The subspecies of moose that live in Alaska are even larger. An Alaskan bull moose can weigh as much as 1800 pounds!

Cow moose are almost as large as the males but they generally weigh less.

About the only time you will see a moose family like this is during the rut or mating season in the fall when the calf of the year tags along during this ritual

In the spring mother moose chases off her last year's calf because she needs all her energies to raise another youngster

Baby moose, called calves, are born in mid to late May and weigh 30 to 40 pounds

Mother moose grunt a variety of messages to their calves: follow me, stay here, it's not time to feed yet, it is time to feed and so on

Do Moose Live In Family Groups?

Moose families consist of a mother and her young. The family may be a single calf, often is two calves and on rare occasions, may be three. An extremely rare case of a moose mother with four calves has been recorded.

While a bull moose shows much adoration as he courts a cow during the fall, he abandons her not long afterwards and never shows any interest in his offspring. In fact, bulls avoid getting near moose babies because they come with one of the most protective mothers in the animal kingdom.

Moose are born from mid to late May. Moose babies stay with their mothers through their first year. But when spring comes again, mother moose break up the family by chasing off their yearlings. A pregnant cow moose needs all her energies to raise another youngster.

An occasional lucky calf whose mother is not pregnant will be permitted to follow mother after its first birthday. But either the mother or an amorous bull will chase it off as a rival when the fall mating season arrives.

Do Moose Talk To Each Other?

Moose grunt to each other in a low-pitched, "uuwhahw", a grunt made by both bulls and cows. It means a different thing depending upon who says it, when they say it, and how they say it. Moose watchers can benefit by knowing the sounds moose make to each other.

During the peak of the rut, bull moose become very vocal as they prowl the woods

A new birth may be a single calf, often is two calves and on rare occasions, may be three

Some might even want to try to bring moose closer by imitating their calls. Only those who really know moose behavior should ever consider this, and then only where it is legal to do so. National Parks in the United States and some other jurisdictions do not permit calling wildlife. Mother moose grunt a variety of messages to their calves: follow me, stay here, it's not time to feed yet, it is time to feed and so on. If you ever watch a cow grunt different messages to her calf, you'll be amazed at how well the little moose understands.

Calves make a bawling sound when they want their mother or are afraid of something in the woods. The bleat can make a mother moose respond in a hurry, and if she thinks that you are the cause for the sound, watch out! They also make grunt-like sounds to talk to their mothers, especially when they're hungry and bored. Mature bulls generally don't vocalize until the fall mating season. Then they grunt either as a greeting or as a signal that they're looking for a mate. During the peak of the rut, bull moose become very vocal as they prowl the woods. Cow moose wail a "weeaahhhoowww" moan-like sound during the rut. It's a signal to bulls that they are in estrus and are willing to mate. Simulating this call can really attract the attention of an amorous bull. If you try it, be sure to have a climbable tree handy!

By fall a young moose will be about two thirds of its size and weight several hundred pounds

How Long Does A Moose Live?

Moose can live twenty years or more unless they succumb to disease, a predator, an accident or a hunter's rifle.

From a start in life at three feet tall, three feet long and from 30 to 40 pounds in weight, a moose grows significantly during its first year. By its first birthday a moose weighs in the 400 pound range and is approaching its adult height. A moose gains weight and mass for the next several years. At five years of age, moose are generally considered to be in their prime.

Do All Moose Have Antlers?

Only the bull moose grow antlers. Bull moose use their antlers to show females that they are healthy breeding stock. They also use them to deter other bulls from messing with their cows during the fall mating season - it's a guy thing, you know?

The moose rut begins in mid September and runs into mid October. Bull moose get pretty cranky as the rut proceeds. In fact, they get downright cantankerous. Some do battle with trees and telephone poles, and some have even attacked parked cars and trucks. It's the time of year to stay well away from any bull moose.

Bull moose display their antlers to deter other bulls from messing with their cows during the fall mating season - it's a guy thing, you know

Two evenly matched bulls will often spar and may actually fight seriously in real head whacking wars. While most moose battles end with one of the bulls running away, some bulls have fought to the death

The velvet that covers the bulls' antlers while they grow during the spring and summer dries and begins to peel away by late August

A bull that feels threatened by the proximity of another will thrash his rack of antlers around, toss his head to display his strength and grunt a challenge while doing so. If you're ever watching a bull moose during the fall and he does that for your benefit, find a tree to climb - fast!

Two evenly matched bulls will often spar and may actually fight seriously in real head whacking wars. While most moose battles end with one of the bulls running away, some bulls have fought to the death for the rights to the pleasures of a cow moose.

A bull moose during the rut can be one of the major animal forces in nature.

What Are Moose Antlers Made Of?

While moose antlers are hardened bone, they actually start out as soft tissue. The outer layer is a fur-covered skin filled with blood vessels, called velvet because of its soft, smooth look. Once the tissue matures and hardens into bone by late August, the velvet dries and begins to peel away. A moose often helps by scraping his antlers against trees or rocks or whatever else suits him. Yearling bulls grow only two small bumps, sometimes even short spikes, by September.

Moose are generally about three years old before they grow forked or branched antlers. Moose five or more years old generally grows the real "racks" - the palmated antlers that most folks think of as moose antlers.

Moose antlers are deciduous: they grow every year, beginning in the spring. The older bulls generally start to grow their antlers earliest. And because they grow antlers faster then the younger moose, they have some pretty awesome antlers by early summer.

A large rack of moose antlers may weigh as much as 60 pounds. A recent record rack from an Alaskan moose weighed 77 pounds!

A bull moose carries his heavy rack of antlers only until the early snows of winter. Then, when he needs to save as much energy as possible to survive this toughest time of the year, the bull will shed his heavy antlers as they loosen and fall off.

Trophy racks are judged partly by the number of "points" that they have. Points must stick out an inch or more from the edge of the antler bowl to be counted. The racks of a mature bull moose may have 20 or more points. Trophy racks are also judged by their spread - the distance between the two outer ends of the pair of antlers. A prime mature bull has a spread that could be 60 inches or more. A Maine moose rack from 1900 measured 71 5/8 inches across - almost 6 feet. The current world's record is from an Alaskan moose that had an 81 - inch spread!

Are Moose Dangerous?

Any animal that weighs half a ton or more, stands seven feet at the shoulder and has its own "bad hair days" at certain times of year certainly can be dangerous.

When I wrote the Maine Moose Watchers Guide in 1993, research of all available information showed no documentation of humans ever being killed by moose except in motor vehicle accidents. That has since changed. Moose stomped two people to death in separate incidents in Alaska in the mid 1990's. Surprisingly, both human fatalities occurred in suburban areas, not out in the big woods as one might imagine.

That's not to say that you should fear moose, but you should have a healthy respect for these large

A bull moose carries his heavy rack of antlers only until the early snows of winter

This bull moose is checking to see if this cow is ready to mate. Notice his broken antler which he probably got from a battle with another bull

and typically quite timid creatures because of their size alone.

You should know that certain moose at certain times of the year require even more respect. Those moose - mothers with calves and aggressive bulls during the fall moose mating season - deserve a lot of space and a wary eye. Mother moose may be the most dangerous land mammal in North America shy of the grizzly bear. They certainly will defend their young from all comers. Should you ever get in a situation where a mother moose perceives you to be a threat: WATCH OUT!

The younger the calf, the more likely you are to encounter aggressive behavior from a mother moose. You don't have to be all that close to a calf to get into trouble. It all depends upon the mother moose and her experience with raising other calves, with people, and perhaps with other animals.

So What Exactly Is A Moose?

A moose is a strange blend of timidity and potential unmatched fury, the true monster of the north woods that could do great damage but rarely does. A moose is a huge hairy beast that thrives by eating aquatic vegetation and twig ends and leaves. A moose is an animal that, while friendly enough when not harassed, could turn on you in the wink of a big old brown moose eye. Because of all that, moose are my favorite wild animal alive on this planet today.

This bull and cow have paired up

A moose is an animal that, while friendly enough when not harassed, could turn on you in the wink of a big old brown moose eye

What A Moose Thinks Of You

What do you suppose a moose thinks when it sees a human?

Why would a moose watcher want to know that? Because, as I tell folks at the moose photography workshops that I teach at L.L. Bean's Outdoor Discovery Schools, try to think as a moose does if you want to get closer for a better view.

How does one think like a moose? First, consider that to a moose all other creatures are either moose or non-moose.

Next, understand that moose see humans as two-legged non-moose. While some moose readily accept the presence of two-legged non-moose, many become wary when they spot one. Some will avoid any contact, especially if they have learned that encounters with two-legged non-moose might cause them harm.

Put yourself in a moose's place. If you were alone in an alley and a car full of strangers drove up and got out and started walking towards you, would it make you nervous?

Moose actually see the world quite poorly. While they have an excellent sense of smell and probably even better hearing, they might not spot a human who is standing still, unless the person is wearing bright clothing in contrast to the forest background.

Some moose readily accept the presence of two-legged non-moose

When moose see a lot of people a lot of the time they become accustomed to them and don't pay much attention

The moose watcher who blends and stands perfectly still when a moose looks at him or her might well evade visual detection at a hundred feet or so. They certainly will at several hundred feet.

Scent detection is a whole other matter. Moose will sniff you out if the wind - even a light breeze - is blowing from you towards them. So if you think a moose you'd like to get close to can't detect you if you're quiet and blend with the scenery, think again. If the moose has the wind advantage, you're moose toast!

Moose similarly hear quite well. They can hear footsteps in the forest - or human voices - a long ways off. If you're watching a moose feeding and it stops and throws a look at the woods and stares at one spot for a long time, expect another moose to emerge from the forest at that spot within a few minutes. I'll bet you won't hear it coming. But your moose did!

Moose rely on both their keen sense of hearing and their sense of smell to protect them from the predators that they share their world with - including the sometimes dreaded two-legged non-moose.

If you're watching a moose feeding and it stops and throws a look at the woods and stares at one spot for a long time, expect another moose to emerge from the forest at that spot

Moose Are Where You Find Them

How do you find a moose to watch? Think about it for a moment. If you were an alien from space and you wanted to watch humans, where might be a good place to look for them? When? How about at a fast food restaurant at noon?

Moose aren't much different. They like to eat regularly too. And like most wild animals, moose often come to feeding sites early in the morning and early in the evening.

Many moose also feed at noontime. In a study of Maine moose in the 1970's the highest use of feeding ponds during spring and summer months was from noon to two in the afternoon.

That study was done before the era of modern moose hunting in Maine, at a time when moose had not felt threatened by humans for over 40 years. With a renewed hunting season, some changes in behavior have been noted by many moose watchers. Many Maine moose have become more wary with increased hunting pressure, and have altered their habits. Hunting pressure on New Hampshire and Vermont moose has to date been more limited.

What does all that mean? It means that moose watchers need to adapt their schedules to the behavior of moose in their region. If significant hunting pressures exist, be sure to get out early in the morning to check moose hotspots. Be quiet and use the approach techniques described elsewhere in this book to get closer to more moose. Those who eat a late supper themselves will also have another chance to see moose as the sun goes down.

The following sub-chapters describe some locations specific to northern New England because moose watching has become such a major tourist activity in those states. The lists were compiled from a variety of sources, including the state wildlife management agencies. Think of any of the roads indicated as places to begin your search from.

In many cases you'll likely find moose in "salt licks" - muddy drainage swales - alongside the road. A really tracked up lick may be a good place to wait for moose. You'll also likely meet some moose right on these roads. Always be sure to drive slowly throughout moose country!

Explore back roads off of the major roads listed here with care - and a good map! And keep in mind that many may be private, paper company owned roads. Be sure to follow the rules of those roads, especially the one about not stopping in the road! And always make room for the logging trucks that use these roads.

Many other opportunities to enjoy moose watching exist if you live near, or travel to other of North America's best moose watching sites, listed below but with less detail. In all moose regions it pays to check at ponds, lakes and bogs where moose foods are plentiful. Scout for their likely presence by looking for sign on the trails: piles of oblong droppings that are deer-like but LARGE; tracks that most often show two toes, are hoof-like and about 6 inches long (occasionally their dew claws - smaller rear toes will also show); and evidence of moose browsing on the forest. While a moose can easily browse from ground to slightly above its eye level, you can generally consider nipped twig ends at your eye level to be made by moose.

Moose watching takes you into some of the most beautiful country there is. This is Maine

And since moose spots can change year to year, it's best to get up-to-date, specific information on any site directly from the managing wildlife authorities of the region.
The following are just some of the better-known places. Many others may produce equally good results for the industrious moose watcher.

Moose will frequent salt licks - muddy drainage swales - alongside the road made by the salt runoff from winter road treatment

Drive slowly throughout moose country because you will likely meet some moose right on the road

This bull has just about completed rubbing all the velvet off his rack in preparation for the rut or mating season. During the rut you may find a moose almost anywhere as they roam to find a mate

Sometimes you can find moose grazing in natural meadows

Maine Moose Hotspots

- Route 201 from The Forks to the Canadian border
- Route 11 from Brownville Junction to Millinocket
- Route 11 from Sherman Station to Fort Kent
- Route 6/15 north from Shirley Corners to Greenville, then west to Jackman
- The Greenville Road from Caribou Lake to Lily Bay State Park
- The Golden Road from Millinocket to the Canadian border (private road)
- Route 16 north from Rangeley to Stratton, and west from Rangeley to New Hampshire
- Route 4 from Phillips to Rangeley
- Route 26 from Grafton Notch State Park to New Hampshire
- The Grand Lake Road from the East Branch of the Penobscot to Shin Pond Village
- Baxter State Park
- The Katahdin Ironworks Region
- The Allagash Wilderness Waterway
- The Jo Mary Forest Region
- The Grand Lake Stream Region

New Hampshire Moose Hotspots

In all moose regions it pays to check at ponds, lakes and bogs where moose foods are plentiful

- Route 3 from Pittsburg to the Canadian border
- Route 16 north from Errol to the Maine border
- Route 26 east from Errol to the Maine border
- Route 302 from Bretton Woods to Twin Mountain
- The Kancamagus Highway, expecially from Blackberry Crossing Campground to the Pass
- Route 110 in the stretch just north of Berlin
- Route 2 from Shelburne to Randolph
- Dirt roads and trails in the Connecticut Lakes Region (includes private roads)
- Dirt roads and trails in the Lake Umbagog area (includes private roads)

Vermont Moose Hotspots

- Route 102 south of Canaan
- Route 114 from Canaan to Island Pond
- Route 2 east from St. Johnsbury to New Hampshire
- Route 105 east from Island Pond to New Hampshire
- Route 114 north from Brighton to Norton
- Route 114 north from Burke to Brighton
- Route 105 west from Bloomfield to Ferdinand
- Route 2 east from Concord to Lunenburg
- The Arthur Davis Wildlife Management Area in Reading

- Victory Bog Wildlife Management Area
- On Route 12, a six mile stretch beginning 14 miles north of Montpelier
- The Railroad Bed east to Bailey Pond, off Lanesboro Road in Marshfield
- Route 73 at Brandon Bog near Rochester

You may watch a spot for hours and then, suddenly, there he is

These moose were found at their feeding site early in the morning and again in the early evening

Other North American Hotspots For Moose Fanatics

Many other great places to watch moose exist throughout North America. In the United States these include: Agassiz National Wildlife Refuge and the Boundary Waters National Park in Minnesota; Denali National Park, pretty much all of the Kenai Peninsula, but especially the Kenai National Moose Refuge in Alaska; Grand Teton National Park in Wyoming; Isle Royale National Park in the Michigan waters of Lake Superior; Rocky Mountain National Park in Colorado, especially near the Grand Lake Entrance; and Yellowstone National Park in Montana and Wyoming.

In Canada, Algonquin Provincial Park in Ontario, Moose Valley Provincial Park in British Columbia, Jasper National Park in Alberta and Gaspesie Provincial Park in Quebec are noted for their moose watching opportunities.

Many other moose watching sites exist in Newfoundland, New Brunswick, British Columbia, and at additional United States locations too numerous to list here. Check with the wildlife management agency of the state or Province in North American moose country where you'd like to go for some ideas on where to enjoy watchable moose.

This beautiful spot is Denali National Park, Alaska

An Alaskan bull in the fall

Here we have a moose at Grand Teton National Park in Wyoming

Bring 'Em Back Alive: Getting Better Moose Photos

Moose can provide great targets for the camera. Because of their size, they often will "fill the frame", even for those with moderate telephoto lenses. To get the best results, keep in mind the following when attempting to photograph a moose:

- Point your camera at something that reflects an average amount of light to set the exposure. Green grass, gray rocks or the blue sky opposite the sun all work well. Adult moose are very dark animals, and if you meter off one, the camera may call for too much exposure. Conversely, if you meter a moose that's in a brightly reflective pond, you run the risk of getting too little exposure of the film if the camera meter picks up much of the pond. Moose calves reflect light just like a gray card: meter them dead on.
- Use a sturdy tripod or some support such as a car door to minimize camera shake with a long telephoto lens. Otherwise, unless you have one of the new stabilizing lenses designed for hand holding at slower shutter speeds, shoot at a shutter speed as fast as the fraction made by the number 1 over the length of the lens. (Example: 1/500 for a 500mm lens).

Photographing moose allows you to enjoy them long after your meeting is over

Those who hike to a backwoods pond and stay quiet while working with a moose generally enjoy better photography opportunities

Photography is catch and release hunting

• Those who hike to a backwoods pond and stay quiet while working with a moose generally enjoy better photography opportunities.
• You can sometimes use a vehicle as a blind to get closer to moose encountered near the road. But as more moose have experienced increased hunting pressures, they have become much more wary than in recent years, and will run from a slowing vehicle. Be sure to shut off the engine to reduce vibration that will impact your photography.
• Always keep in mind that mother moose are very protective and that bull moose in the fall are often aggressive. Use common sense - no photograph is worth endangering yourself or your wild subject.

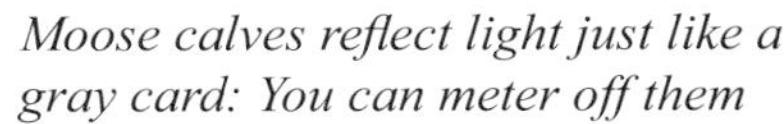

Moose calves reflect light just like a gray card: You can meter off them

Be on the lookout for some unusual shots. This guy looks like he's walking on water

Sometimes it's fun to snap the shot at the moment he lifts his head out of the water

May We Always Have Moose

While moose provide many with the thrill of the hunt, not to mention a lot of meat for the freezer, moose watching is compatible with the balanced sharing of this valuable wildlife resource. Moose watching provides a wonderful opportunity for people to connect with the natural world. I never really appreciated just how much until I got the following letter from a moose watching fan:

"I don't know if you remember me but I e-mailed you a while back about places to check in Vermont. I thought I'd let you know that we had a great year last year. My daughter, who is autistic, and I saw 75 moose! It was a new record for us, up from 47 the year before.

We spent a lot of time in the Northeast Kingdom and also in Moose Alley in New Hampshire. My daughter will come and get me at 3 a.m. every Saturday morning so we can get there before dawn.

We have started hiking in and have found several ponds and boggy areas off the beaten path. This gives us views of moose away from the road and other people scaring them off. I have been able to let the moose get comfortable with my being around. This allows me to sometimes take pictures over periods up to half an hour. It makes me happy to not be such a threat that they run off quickly.

This year, when we made our new record of moose sightings, my daughter was so excited that she almost couldn't contain herself! She was bouncing around in the truck and saying, 'We made a new record! Slap me five!' I had to stop because I couldn't stop my tears from coming."

That about says it all, doesn't it? May we always have moose!

Moose watching provides a wonderful opportunity for people to connect with the natural world

Hiking can help you find moose off the beaten path, away from the road where other people can scare them off. Look for ponds and boggy areas where moose love to hang out

When a moose gets comfortable with your being around, it's a wonderful feeling

"May we always have Moose to watch"